DANVERS TOWNSHIP LIBRARY

A31300 082735

24521

JB
EAR

Raatma, Lucia
Amelia Earhart

AR 6.4

DATE DUE			
APR 05 2004			

DANVERS TWP. LIBRARY
105 South West Street
Danvers, Illinois 61732
Phone: 963-4269

MEDIALOG INC
Butler, KY 41006

D1383518

AMELIA EARHART

By Lucia Raatma

DANVERS TWP. LIBRARY
105 South West Street
Danvers, Illinois 61732
Phone: 963-4269

WORLD ALMANAC® LIBRARY

Please visit our web site at: www.worldalmanaclibrary.com
For a free color catalog describing World Almanac® Library's list of high-quality books
and multimedia programs, call 1-800-848-2928 (USA) or 1-800-461-9120 (Canada).
World Almanac® Library's Fax: (414) 332-3567.

Library of Congress Cataloging-in-Publication Data

Raatma, Lucia.
    Amelia Earhart / by Lucia Raatma.
      p. cm. — (Trailblazers of the modern world)
    Includes bibliographical references and index.
    Summary: Describes the life of the pilot who, in 1932, was the first woman to fly alone across the Atlantic Ocean,
and who was later lost at sea while attempting to fly around the world.
    ISBN 0-8368-5063-7 (lib. bdg.)
    ISBN 0-8368-5223-0 (softcover)
    1. Earhart, Amelia, 1897-1937—Juvenile literature. 2. Women air pilots—United States—Biography—Juvenile
literature. 3. Air pilots—United States—Biography—Juvenile literature. [1. Earhart, Amelia, 1897-1937. 2. Air
pilots. 3. Women—Biography.] I. Title. II. Series.
TL540.E3R32   2001
629.13'092—dc21
[B]   2001034181

This North American edition first published in 2001 by
World Almanac® Library
330 West Olive Street, Suite 100
Milwaukee, WI 53212 USA

This U.S. edition © 2001 by World Almanac® Library.

An Editorial Directions book
Editor: E. Russell Primm III
Designer and page production: Ox and Company
Photo researcher: Dawn Friedman
Indexer: Timothy Griffin
Proofreader: Neal Durando
World Almanac® Library art direction: Karen Knutson
World Almanac® Library editor: Jacqueline Laks Gorman
World Almanac® Library production: Susan Ashley and Jessica L. Yanke

Photo credits: AP/Wide World Photos, cover; Hulton/Archive/American Stock, 4; AP/Wide World Photos, 5, 6;
Hulton/Archive, 7; Corbis/Bettmann, 8 top; Hulton/Archive, 8 bottom; Corbis/Underwood & Underwood/George
Rinhart, 10; Corbis/Rykoff Collection/The American Art Publishing Co., 11; AP/Wide World Photos/John T. Daniels, 12;
Corbis/Bettmann, 13; Hulton/Archive/APA, 14; Corbis, 15, 17; Hulton/ArchivePopperfoto, 18; Hulton/Archive/Hulton
Getty/J. Gaiger, 20; Hulton/Archive/Hulton Getty, 21; Corbis/Underwood & Underwood/George Rinhart, 22, 23;
Hulton/Archive/Hulton Getty, 24; AP/Wide World Photos, 25 left, 25 right; Corbis/Bettmann, 26; AP/Wide World
Photos, 28; Hulton/Archive, 29; AP/Wide World Photos, 31; Hulton/Archive, 33; AP/Wide World Photos, 34;
Corbis/Bettmann, 35; AP/Wide World Photos, 36; Corbis, 37 top; AP/Wide World Photos, 37 bottom;
Hulton/Archive/APA, 38; Corbis, 39; Hulton/Archive/Sam Sargent, 40 top; AP/Wide World Photos, 40 bottom; Corbis, 41
top; AP/Wide World Photos, 41 bottom; Hulton/Archive/G. Swersey, 43 top; Hulton/Archive/Lori Borgman, 43 bottom.

All rights reserved. No part of this book may be reproduced, stored in a retrieval system, or transmitted in any form
or by any means, electronic, mechanical, photocopying, recording, or otherwise without the prior written permission
of the copyright holder.

Printed in the United States of America

1 2 3 4 5 6 7 8 9 05 04 03 02 01

TABLE of CONTENTS

CHAPTER 1

EYES ON THE SKY

When people talk about the early days of flying, Amelia Earhart is always mentioned. She was one of the first female pilots and the first woman to cross the Atlantic by airplane. Her accomplishments promoted aviation— the business of flying. Because of her achievements as a pilot, airplane flight became more popular, more common, and more accepted.

Amelia Earhart did much to change the world of aviation.

AN EARLY FEMINIST

Amelia Earhart's efforts also helped the women's movement. She was a **feminist**—a believer in equal rights for women—and she believed that women could do everything that men do. Amelia often wore slacks instead of dresses, and she said that marriage should be an equal partnership. She even kept her own name after she married, an action considered strange at that time.

A NATIONAL HEROINE WITH A TRAGIC END

During her years of fame, Amelia Earhart was loved by the media and by people all over the world. Women sought her advice, and little girls aspired to grow up to be just like her. To the people of the United States, she was brave and intelligent as well as glamorous.

Earhart was seen by many as glamorous and intelligent.

This remarkable pilot is of course remembered today for her famous flights, but she is also remembered for the mystery surrounding her last mission. Her hope had been to complete a round-the-world journey, but somewhere in the Pacific, her airplane disappeared. To this day, no one is sure what became of the young woman. No doubt that mystery makes the story of her life even more interesting.

CHAPTER 2

BEGINNINGS

From the very beginning, Amelia Earhart had a mind of her own. She liked all kinds of adventure, and her parents, Edwin and Amy Earhart, encouraged her to try new things. They liked her spirit of independence and felt sure that it would help her throughout her life.

Edwin Earhart came from a poor family in Atchison, Kansas, but he fell in love with Amy Otis, a wealthy young woman and the daughter of a respected Atchison judge. Edwin Earhart worked hard as a lawyer because he wanted to gain the approval of his father-in-law, Amy's father.

The house in Atchison, Kansas, where Amelia Earhart was born

When Amy was pregnant, she lived with her parents in their large home while Edwin was away on business. There, Amelia Mary Earhart was born on July 24, 1897. About two years later, her sister, Muriel, was born. The girls were best friends throughout their childhood and remained close all their lives.

Amelia (right) and her sister, Muriel

EARLY ADVENTURE

Amelia and Muriel spent a great deal of time at their grandparents' home. They often stayed there when their mother joined their father in his travels. The girls had everything they needed, including good clothes and good schools, but they loved adventure too. They explored the property around their grandparents' house and played along the banks of the Mississippi River.

The sisters were **tomboys** in many ways. For instance, they liked fishing and playing ball. They even wore bloomers—odd-looking trousers worn by athletic girls in those days. Amy and Edwin Earhart encouraged their daughters' curiosity and energy, though some people thought the girls were a bit too active.

To Fly Like a Bird

As a child, Amelia enjoyed both reading and writing. Sometimes her daydreams turned into poetry:

*I watch the birds flying all day long
And I want to fly too.
Don't they look down sometimes, I wonder,
And wish they were me
When I'm going to the circus with my daddy?*

Amelia at age seven

Young Amelia Earhart was smart and independent.

Amelia enjoyed much of her childhood, but as she got older, life became more difficult. For years, her father tried to live up to the high standards set by Amelia's grandfather, but those expectations were hard on him. He never seemed to make enough money or be successful enough, so he always felt that his father-in-law did not approve of him.

Edwin Earhart made a few bad business decisions that lost money. Then he started having a problem with alcohol, drinking too much. He lost a job and had to find another, and then he lost that job. This pattern repeated itself over and over, and each time he got a new job, the family had to move. As a result, Amelia and Muriel went to many different schools and lived in many different places. After a while, Amy Earhart lost patience with her husband. She left Edwin and took Amelia and Muriel to Chicago.

At that time, Amelia was in high school. She was upset by her father's situation, and she was also upset that her parents were separated. These feelings made her fearful to make friends, so she kept to herself. Amelia was a good student and studied hard. She didn't worry much about what other people thought of her. Instead, she was independent and self-reliant. She played on the basketball team but otherwise stayed away from groups.

A Devoted Daughter

In spite of the problems Edwin Earhart had, Amelia thought the world of him. She was impressed by his intelligence, and later in life she wrote:

I thought my father must have read everything and, of course, therefore, knew everything. He could define the hardest words as well as the dictionary, and we used to try to trip him and he to bewilder us. I still have a letter he wrote me beginning, "Dear parallelepipedon," which sent me scurrying for a definition.

NEW STARTS

Over the next few years, Amelia's father took control of his problems, and his condition improved a great deal. He stopped drinking, and he started his own law practice. Amy Earhart returned to Kansas City to live with her husband and brought her daughters with her.

Amelia was eager to go to college, but there were money problems. Amy Earhart had inherited a large sum when her mother died. However, Amy's mother had worried about Edwin's drinking habits, so she made unusual arrangements for the money. It was placed in a bank account for twenty years, or until Edwin died. She wanted to be sure that he did not get access to the money and spend it on alcohol. Since Amelia and Muriel both needed the inheritance to continue their schooling, Amy took the matter to court. The judge awarded the money to the Earharts, and finally the girls were able to get on with their education.

Amelia chose the Ogontz School, a college preparatory school just outside Philadelphia. In the meantime,

Earhart's graduation photo from the Ogontz School

Muriel headed to Toronto, Canada, to attend St. Margaret's. At Ogontz, Amelia enjoyed all sorts of subjects and pastimes. She went to the theater and to various lectures, and she rode horses and played tennis. She also began doing volunteer work for the Red Cross. For Amelia, her time at Ogontz proved to be another grand adventure.

ON HER OWN

During her Christmas vacation in 1917, Amelia Earhart visited Muriel in Canada, where she saw many men who had been wounded while fighting in World War I (1914–1918). Canada had been involved in the war since 1914, but the United States had entered the conflict only months before. Some of the men Earhart saw were blind and some had lost a leg or an arm. Suddenly, the war became very real to her, and she wanted to help somehow.

HELPING THE SICK

The following spring, Earhart moved to Toronto, Canada. She took a course offered by the Red Cross and became a nurse's aide at Spadina Military Hospital. There she cleaned and worked in the kitchen, in addition to spending time with the wounded soldiers and getting to know them. Some of the men she met were pilots, and they talked about the airplanes they had been flying. At first, Earhart was not impressed with the planes she heard about, but the idea of flying had been planted in her mind.

The war ended in 1918, but working in the hospital had affected Earhart. She decided she wanted to go back to school to study medicine. She moved to New York City and enrolled at Columbia University.

Earhart enrolled at Columbia University in 1919.

The Wright Brothers

On December 17, 1903, Wilbur and Orville Wright made history. They had built an airplane and decided it was time to test it out. At Kitty Hawk, North Carolina, Orville Wright piloted the plane as it lifted off. He flew for a total of twelve seconds and for a distance of 120 feet (37 meters). It may have been a short flight, but it was the first flight in history for a gasoline-powered plane!

The Wright Brothers continued to build airplanes, improving on the design each time. Soon the planes could fly farther, and as the years passed, flying became more common for people all over the world.

CHANGE OF DIRECTION

After studying medicine for a year, Earhart visited her parents, who were then living in California. While she was there, she went to her first air show with her father. At these events, pilots entertained the audience by performing stunts. Air shows had become popular after World War I, and crowds of people attended them. As

High-Flying Stunts

Flying airplanes was still a novel idea in the 1920s. The stunt pilots who performed at air shows took lots of risks, making loops and rolls in their airplanes. Wing-walkers thrilled onlookers by walking out on the wings of an airplane in flight, and other daredevils made dramatic parachute jumps from planes. The air shows were dangerous, but they definitely were exciting.

Amelia watched the talented pilots, she started thinking about flying.

A few days later, Earhart took her first ride in an airplane. She paid the pilot $1 for ten minutes over Los Angeles. From that moment on, everything—including all her plans for herself—changed. She remembered, "By the time I had gotten two or three hundred feet off the ground, I knew I had to fly."

Women had just earned the right to vote when Earhart was learning to fly planes.

A DETERMINED WOMAN

After that first flight, Earhart was hooked—she knew she wanted to learn to fly. Lessons were very expensive, but she was determined to be a pilot. This was an unusual goal for a woman at this time in history, when women still had limited rights and a relatively narrow role in society. In the United States in 1920, women had just won the right to vote. Women were expected to be wives and mothers, not pilots, but Amelia Earhart did not let such notions stop her. She decided to stay in California and pursue her interest in flying.

WOMAN IN THE COCKPIT

To pay for her many flying lessons, Amelia Earhart immediately got a job at the local telephone company. She worked hard all week so that she could spend time in airplanes on the weekend.

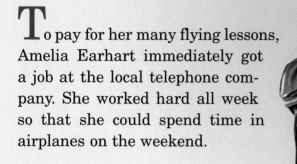

Earhart in her flying gear

LEARNING TO FLY

Earhart's flight instructor, Neta Snook, was the first woman to graduate from the Curtiss School of Aviation. When Earhart flew the airplane, Snook sat behind her so that she could watch all that her student did. Earhart learned to take off and land, and she practiced techniques for surviving emergencies. Earhart also spent time talking with other pilots and asking all kinds of questions.

During her lessons, Earhart wore slacks, boots, goggles, and a leather jacket just like the men. She dressed that way because these clothes were practical for flying. In those days, some people thought it was a strange way for a woman to dress, but Earhart was never bothered by what other people thought. In the summer of 1922, when Earhart earned her pilot's license, there were only about a dozen female pilots in the world.

The Kinner Airster

Amelia Earhart's first airplane was a bright-yellow **biplane** called a Kinner Airster. She bought it with money she had saved and with contributions from her family. She was proud to have her very own plane, and she flew as often as she could. Amy Earhart even commented that her daughter treated the plane like a pet. "It was like a favorite pony. We said goodnight to it and patted its nose and almost fed it apples."

SETTING A RECORD

One afternoon, Earhart invited her father and sister to an air show. They were unaware that Earhart was going to perform there—let alone that she was going to try to set a new **altitude** record. At that air show, Earhart soared 14,000 feet (4,270 m)—the highest altitude a woman had ever flown! The record was broken a few weeks later by someone else, but Earhart thoroughly enjoyed her accomplishment.

A CHANGE IN COURSE

Amelia Earhart loved to fly, but there were no paying jobs for a woman pilot. In the mid-1920s, she had to decide how she would support herself.

By this time, her parents had finally divorced, and Muriel was going to attend college in Massachusetts. Earhart decided to sell her plane and buy a car instead. She drove her mother and sister from California to

Boston. Then Earhart began looking for a job in this new city, and she tried to settle into her new home.

Before long, Earhart found a position at a community center, working with immigrant families. She taught English, played with the children, and organized social events. But while she put a lot of effort into the job, her mind was still in the sky.

Amelia's mother, Amy (left), and sister, Muriel, in the 1920s

Charles Lindbergh's Historic Flight

On May 21, 1927, aviator Charles Lindbergh flew from New York to Paris. This trip was the first nonstop **solo** flight across the Atlantic Ocean. Lindbergh's flight drew a great deal of attention, and he was instantly famous. Photos of him standing next to his plane, *Spirit of St. Louis*, appeared in newspapers all over the world. In the years to come, Lindbergh worked to make flying more popular as a form of transportation.

HER BIG CHANCE

While she was in Boston, Earhart joined the National Aeronautic Association. She flew whenever she could and even invested in a local airport. These activities kept her known in the flying world, and one day that recognition paid off.

She got a phone call from Captain Hilton Railey, a public relations executive who represented Amy Guest, a wealthy woman with big ideas. Mrs. Guest, inspired by Charles Lindbergh's historic flight across the Atlantic, felt that a woman should accomplish the same feat. She wanted a woman to fly from the United States to England, and she hired Hilton Railey to find the perfect woman for the trip. An excited Amelia Earhart agreed to meet with him.

CHAPTER 5

MAKING HISTORY

Earhart with Captain Railey

Hilton Railey found Amelia Earhart to be smart and charming, and he also noted that she slightly resembled Charles Lindbergh! They both had light hair and a casual grin.

Earhart then met with a committee of men that included publisher George Palmer Putnam. Shortly after that meeting, she received a letter saying that she had been chosen to make the historic flight. Amelia Earhart was going to fly across the Atlantic!

JUST A PASSENGER

As the plans for the flight were made, one thing became clear. Earhart was to be the commander of the flight, but not the pilot. Two men—Wilmer Stultz and Louis Gordon—would do the actual flying. Earhart was naturally disappointed about this, but she had no experience with a big plane like the one they would be using. The plane, named *Friendship*, was bright orange, and its golden wings spanned 72 feet (22 m). It had **pontoons**, which are used for floating in water. Even though the plane was new and well equipped, this would be a dangerous flight. Nevertheless, Earhart was happy and excited.

As preparations were made, the flight was kept secret. The original plan was to take off from Boston in May 1928, a year after Lindbergh had made his historic flight. However, bad weather pushed the date back.

ACROSS THE ATLANTIC

Finally, on June 3, 1928, Earhart and the two men flew from Boston to Trepassey Bay in Newfoundland, where they planned to take on more fuel. As soon as they took off, George Putnam met with reporters and informed them that a woman had just begun a flight across the Atlantic.

However, once in Newfoundland, they ran into more bad weather, and this time they were delayed for two weeks. It was a difficult time. Everyone was getting bored, and they also felt the pressure to complete a successful flight.

On June 17, the plane took to the air again. Earhart read the maps and made entries in the **logbook**. She recorded information about the weather, their speed, their altitude, and their position. The crew seemed to be on course, but later that night their radio stopped working. They could no longer communicate with anyone on the ground.

Amelia Earhart on a stopover in Newfoundland

While Amelia flew across the Atlantic, her mother listened to news of the flight on her radio.

The next morning, the pilots—unable to maintain radio contact—could only guess their location. They were over the Atlantic and hoped they were still headed in the right direction. Fuel was running low, so Stultz just kept heading in the direction he thought would lead to land.

Finally, after twenty hours and forty minutes, the crew spotted land. Relieved and exhausted, they landed the plane. They were in Burry Port, Wales. It was not their intended destination, but they had crossed the Atlantic successfully.

IN THE PRESS

Once on the ground, Amelia Earhart was immediately famous. Reporters wanted to know everything about her. She was upset that the two men she had flown with were almost ignored by the press. Though they had actually flown the plane, she was getting all the attention. Apparently, a woman flying across the Atlantic—even as a passenger—was important news.

The reporters gave Earhart the nickname "Lady Lindy" (after Charles Lindbergh). President Calvin Coolidge sent a **cable** congratulating her on the flight, and she joined the two pilots in a **ticker-tape parade** in New York City.

opposite: Earhart with Wilmer Stultz (left) and Louis Gordon (right) during their ticker-tape parade

Parading down Broadway

Ticker-tape parades in New York City are a longtime tradition. The ticker tape refers to the small pieces of paper showered on the guests of honor, a bit like confetti. These parades mark special events in U.S. history. Charles Lindbergh and many astronauts celebrated their historic flights with similar parades. New York baseball teams that win the World Series have also been honored with ticker-tape parades.

Amelia Earhart gave many talks about her historic flight.

AUTHOR AND CELEBRITY

Amelia Earhart was in great demand after the flight, as people asked her to make appearances and talk about her adventures. George Putnam became her business manager and did all he could to keep her name in the newspapers. He enjoyed the fame she was getting.

Earhart also agreed to write *20 Hours, 40 Minutes*, a book about the flight. George Putnam published the book and worked on its publicity too. This all earned Earhart enough money to purchase her own plane, so she bought one called an Avian Moth and finally had her freedom again.

After finishing the book, Earhart flew from New York to California, where she attended the National Air Races and visited her father. Once she returned to New York, she had set another mark.

She was the first woman to make a round-trip solo flight across the United States.

Back in New York, Earhart worked on promoting her book. She was also offered a writing job with *Cosmopolitan* magazine. She wrote articles about the safety of flying and encouraged other women to fly. Readers loved her column, and she got lots of fan mail.

WOMEN IN THE AIR

One of Earhart's main goals had always been to support other women in aviation, so she was happy to participate in a cross-country race for women pilots. In the summer of 1929, she bought a Lockheed Vega—a more powerful plane—and flew to California for the race.

Earhart was joined by nineteen other pilots, including Ruth Nichols and Louise Thaden. Fifteen pilots completed the flight, flying from Los Angeles to Cleveland.

Ruth Nichols (left) and Louise Thaden (right) joined Earhart and others in forming the Ninety-Nines.

An original group of the
Ninety-Nines

The Ninety-Nines

Today the Ninety-Nines is an international organization with approximately six thousand members. Members come from thirty-five countries, but most are from the United States. The group follows this mission statement:

Promote world fellowship through flight.

Provide networking and scholarship opportunities for women and aviation education in the community.

Preserve the history of women in aviation.

Thaden came in first, while Earhart placed third. The event was very successful, and after it was over, the women met and formed the Ninety-Nines. The name refers to the first members—ninety-nine licensed women pilots. This organization is now famous for all it has done to promote women pilots. Earhart was elected the group's first president.

Throughout her life and by using this organization, Earhart urged women to follow their dreams. She respected other women pilots and inspired many to get their licenses. She once said, "The more women fly, the more who become pilots, the quicker we will be recognized as an important factor in aviation."

CHAPTER 6

FAME AND FORTUNE

Amelia Earhart used her fame to promote aviation. She joined the Transcontinental Air Transport and served as an adviser to that organization. Her main responsibility was convincing women that flying was safe. She wanted them to feel comfortable, not only as airplane pilots, but also as passengers.

After many tries, George Putnam convinced Amelia Earhart to marry him.

TIME FOR ROMANCE

Meanwhile, as they worked together, Amelia Earhart and George Putnam had become very close. He seemed to understand her need for adventure, and she appreciated all the support and advice he gave her. When they first met, Putnam was married, but in 1929 he got a divorce. Shortly thereafter, GP (as Amelia called him) asked her to marry him.

At first, AE (as GP called her) said no. She did not want to get married because she had seen how unhappy marriages such as her parents' could be, and she did not want to be tied down. However, GP refused to give up. He kept asking her to be

Putnam and Earhart had a strong marriage based on equality and mutual respect.

his wife, and finally he convinced her that their marriage would be special. She could still be a pilot, and she could still have her freedom. That, he promised, would not change. After the sixth proposal, AE agreed. She married GP on February 7, 1931.

A WORKING MARRIAGE

Putnam was true to his word about their marriage. When they became husband and wife, he and Earhart continued to work together. He promoted her career, and she traveled all over the country giving talks. Soon she began speaking about things other than flying. For example, she talked about relationships between men and women.

She once said, "Marriage is a mutual responsibility and I cannot see why husbands shouldn't share in the responsibility of the home." Such ideas were quite unusual in the 1930s, but Earhart spoke out for women's rights and disagreed with any kind of unequal treatment for women.

MARKETING AMELIA EARHART

One of George Putnam's projects was developing a line of Amelia Earhart clothing and luggage. The clothing was marketed "for the woman who lives actively" and included loose-fitting slacks and jackets with zippers and big pockets. More formal and elegant kinds of clothing were also offered. *Vogue* magazine featured a two-page spread on the Amelia Earhart line. It was sold in thirty cities at exclusive stores such as Macy's and Marshall Field's.

A SOLO FLIGHT

Throughout all this, something was bothering Earhart. She had always been disturbed because she got so much attention for a flight she didn't even pilot. For years, she had wanted to make a flight across the Atlantic on her own. She wanted to prove that a woman could do it.

When she mentioned the idea to Putnam, he was very supportive. So she began serious training and did all she could to prepare for the long flight. Finally, May 1932 was set as the time to go. It was exactly five years after Lindbergh's flight, and Putnam saw the date as great publicity.

A cheering crowd in Londonderry, Northern Ireland

On May 20, Earhart took off in her Lockheed Vega from Harbor Grace, Newfoundland. Not long after the flight began, she experienced problems. Her **altimeter** stopped working, so she didn't know how high up in the air she was. Then she ran into a storm and had a hard time seeing, but she decided to go on. The plane vibrated and, at one point, a small fire started in its exhaust. No doubt Amelia was scared, but she used her experience and intelligence to continue the flight. Nothing could stop Earhart.

Many hours later, on May 21, Earhart saw land. She set her plane down on the green grass of a farm and was told she was in Londonderry, Northern Ireland. She had done it! Amelia Earhart had become the first woman to fly solo across the Atlantic.

Courage

Amelia Earhart wrote the following poem when she was a young woman. It says a great deal about her sense of adventure.

Courage is the price which life exacts for granting peace.
The soul that knows it not, knows no release
From little things;

Knows not the livid loneliness of fear,
Nor mountain heights, where bitter joy can hear
The sound of wings.

How can life grant us boon of living, compensate
For dull grey ugliness and pregnant hate
Unless we dare

The soul's dominion? Each time we make a choice, we pay
With courage to behold the restless day,
And count it fair.

Earhart being honored at City Hall in New York City, June 1932

CELEBRITY STATUS

The successful flight made Earhart more famous than ever. She and her husband traveled all over the world, and they were entertained by royalty and government leaders. Back in the United States, Earhart was awarded the Distinguished Flying Cross, making her the first

Flying was great fun for Earhart, and she encouraged other women to try it.

Women Pilots

In *For the Fun of It*, Earhart describes women pilots this way:

Of course, they are as different as individuals from any other group. There are slim ones and plump ones and quiet ones and those who talk all the time. They're large and small, young and old, about half the list are married and many of these have children. . . . They are simply thoroughly normal girls and women who happen to have taken up flying rather than golf, swimming, or **steeplechasing**.

woman to receive such an honor. She was also given the National Geographic Society's Special Gold Medal. After the flight, Earhart wrote *For the Fun of It*, another book that George Putnam published. The book talked about aviation and the growing number of women in the field.

Amelia Earhart with First Lady Eleanor Roosevelt

MORE FLIGHTS

In the following years, Earhart made many more flights. She became the first person to fly solo from Hawaii to California and then flew from California to Mexico City and on to New Jersey, setting distance records along the way. She was often a guest at the White House, and once—after learning that First Lady Eleanor Roosevelt had never flown—Earhart borrowed a plane and took Mrs. Roosevelt for a spin. Amelia Earhart had become the unofficial ambassador of aviation.

CHAPTER 7

AROUND THE WORLD

opposite: *Flying Laboratory* was the name of Earhart's Lockheed Electra.

Earhart with movie stars Douglas Fairbanks and Mary Pickford

In the early 1930s, Amelia Earhart and George Putnam moved to California. There they spent time with celebrated movie stars such as Mary Pickford and Douglas Fairbanks, and Earhart became friends with Will Rogers, a popular and well-known humorist. She enjoyed the landscape and the warm weather. For Earhart and Putnam, life was very good.

AT PURDUE UNIVERSITY

In 1935, Earhart accepted a part-time position at Purdue University in Indiana. She shared her knowledge about flying with female students there and advised the university on a number of aviation issues. She also served as a women's career counselor. College officials were so pleased with Earhart's contributions that they gave her a new plane—a brand-new, silver Lockheed Electra. It could fly farther than any plane Earhart had ever piloted. She named it the *Flying Laboratory*, and she began talking about flying around the world.

Tragedy in the Arctic

Wiley Post (at right) was one of Amelia Earhart's flying friends and an experienced pilot who had already flown around the world. In August 1935, he and humorist Will Rogers (left) set off on a flight to the Arctic Circle. Unfortunately, their plane got caught in a fog over Alaska. The plane crashed, and both men were killed. Although Earhart mourned the loss of her two friends, she did not let this tragedy keep her from flying.

Amelia Earhart began to plan her round-the-world flight. Some people thought she was taking too big a risk, but nothing shook Earhart's determination. Her original route was to be from east to west, so she planned to fly from California to Hawaii, then to Australia, Saudi Arabia, and Africa. From there she would fly to Brazil and then back to the United States.

Earhart hired three men to work with her—Harry Manning and Fred Noonan as **navigators** and Paul Mantz as an adviser. On March 17, 1937, the group took off from California and headed for Hawaii, where they stopped to rest and refuel. Bad weather kept them on the ground for a few days. Then on March 20, they prepared to take off again.

Earhart with Harry Manning (center) and Fred Noonan (right)

Halfway down the runway, Earhart realized there was a problem. The plane was not going fast enough to take off. Then the aircraft turned sharply. Earhart struggled to regain control, but the landing gear broke off and gasoline spilled out. Earhart quickly turned off the engines, which kept the plane from catching fire. No one was hurt in the accident, but the plane was badly damaged. The plane was shipped to Los Angeles for repairs, and Earhart's round-the-world flight was postponed.

Inspecting the damage after Earhart's accident in Hawaii

ANOTHER TRY

By May, when Earhart planned another attempt, weather patterns would have changed. So, as she waited for her plane to be fixed, she reconsidered her route. She decided that a route from west to east would make more sense. Her plan was to begin in California, then fly to Florida. From there, she would continue to South America, cross the Atlantic to Africa, and then go on to Asia. The next part of the trip would be to Australia, then New Guinea, Hawaii, and back to California.

Today's Airplanes

The airplanes we fly in today are quite different from the planes Amelia Earhart used in the 1920s and 1930s. Today's planes have state-of-the-art navigational devices. Air-traffic controllers can talk to pilots throughout their flights, and their towers are equipped with high-tech **radar**.

Autopilot was not available in Amelia Earhart's day. She had to remain alert and in control of the plane at all times, and many of the flights she attempted were long and exhausting. Today, planes can also fly much faster than those used at that time.

Repairing *Flying Laboratory* turned out to be very expensive, as much as $25,000. George Putnam raised money to pay the bills, and he and Earhart used all their savings as well.

Paul Mantz served as Earhart's flight adviser.

In the meantime, Harry Manning had to leave the project, but Fred Noonan stayed on as Earhart's navigator and Paul Mantz continued to advise her. Mantz was extremely upset when he saw that she had removed a large radio antenna and a telegraph key from the plane. Earhart thought the antenna was unnecessary, and since neither she nor Noonan knew anything about **Morse code**, she felt that the telegraph was **superfluous** too. Mantz tried to convince her to keep the devices because,

George Putnam helped Earhart plan the ill-fated round-the-world trip.

without them, people on the ground would find it harder to communicate with Earhart in flight. Unfortunately, she paid little attention to his concern.

On May 20, 1937, Earhart and Noonan took off from California. When they stopped for more fuel in Arizona, the engine caught fire, but mechanics were able to fix the plane overnight. The two then headed for Florida. In Miami, they had the plane's engine rechecked and made more preparations for the long flight.

On June 1, they set out from Miami. As they flew, news of their long flight circled the world. By June 6, Earhart and Noonan had reached Brazil and, by June 10, they were in Africa. The next part of the flight was over Saudi

Earhart and Noonan shortly before they disappeared

Arabia and the Arabian Sea. On June 17, they flew over India, where they had to endure the heavy rains of the **monsoon** season. Then they went on to Australia and New Guinea. By June 30, Earhart had flown 22,000 miles (35,400 kilometers). Only 7,000 miles (11,260 km) remained, but it was the hardest part of the journey. Their next stop was to be Howland Island, a tiny island in the Pacific Ocean. Howland was only 2 miles long (3.2 km) and 0.5 miles (0.8 km) wide—hard to find in the huge Pacific.

Earhart and Noonan took off from New Guinea on July 2. Earhart was nervous about this part of the flight, and she was also worried about her navigator. Noonan, who was anxious about the flight, had begun drinking too much. Earhart had known about his problems with alcohol, but she believed he was good at his job.

Three U.S. Navy ships had been sent to the Pacific Ocean to communicate with the *Flying Laboratory*. The ships would provide signals and guide the plane to Howland Island. Seven hours after she and Noonan took off, Earhart sent a transmission that reported her position. She was on course.

The next morning, Earhart was heard on her radio reporting that the weather was cloudy. An hour later, she told radio operators she was circling the island. Apparently, she thought she was over Howland Island. However, five hours later, she sent another message that she was still searching for the island. The ships sent her message after message, but Earhart never responded. There may have been some confusion about the signals, or she may not have received the messages because she had removed the radio antenna. Whatever the reason, no one ever heard from Amelia Earhart again.

The U.S. Navy sent out a huge rescue crew to search for the fliers or the plane. The search went on for weeks, but nothing was ever found.

WHAT SHE LEFT BEHIND

After Amelia Earhart's disappearance, rumors spread about her fate. Japan had many military bases in the Pacific at that time, so some people suggested that the Japanese had imagined Earhart was spying on them and captured her. Other people made up stories about Earhart and Noonan living together on a tropical island. It may be that Earhart merely lost her way, ran out of fuel, and crashed. People continue to search for the remains of her plane even today.

No matter what really happened, Amelia Earhart's work remains alive today. She wanted to prove that women were as capable as men, and she was successful. She made progress in aviation as well as in women's rights. Her independence and free spirit inspired both men and women all over the world.

Before she left on her last flight, Earhart gave George Putnam a letter that he was to open only if she didn't return. In the letter, she said many things, including this:

> *Please know that I am quite aware of the hazards.... Women must try to do things as men have tried. When they fail, their failure must be but a challenge to others.*

Thanks to Earhart's success, many women are pilots today.

Throughout her life, Amelia Earhart was eager to embrace new challenges.

TIMELINE

1897	Amelia Earhart is born on July 24 in Atchison, Kansas
1903	Wright brothers make their historic flight
1917	Earhart enters the Ogontz School
1918	Becomes a nurse's aide in a Toronto hospital
1919	Begins taking medical courses at Columbia University
1920	Moves to California and develops a serious interest in flying
1922	Earns her pilot's license
1926	Moves to Boston and works in a community center
1927	Charles Lindbergh makes his solo flight across the Atlantic
1928	On June 18, Earhart becomes the first woman to fly across the Atlantic Ocean; in September, becomes the first woman to make a round-trip solo flight across the United States
1929	Becomes the first president of the Ninety-Nines
1931	Marries George Palmer Putnam on February 7
1932	On May 21, becomes the first woman to make a solo flight across the Atlantic Ocean
1935	Accepts a part-time position at Purdue University
1937	Undertakes a round-the-world flight; disappears over the Pacific Ocean on July 3

altimeter: a device that measures the height of a plane above sea level

altitude: the height of a plane (or any object) in the air

autopilot: a device that allows a plane to fly itself for brief periods of time

biplane: an aircraft with two sets of wings, usually one above the other

cable: a message sent via underground telegraph lines

cockpit: the part of an airplane where the pilot sits

feminist: a person who works to further the cause of equality for women

logbook: a record book containing details of a ship's voyage or an airplane's flight

monsoon: a strong wind across the Indian Ocean and southern Asia that brings heavy rains

Morse code: a system of long and short sounds—used to transmit messages

navigators: people who track the position, distance, and course for an airplane

pontoons: floats that allow an airplane to land on water

radar: a system that uses radio waves to locate objects

solo: alone

steeplechasing: participating in a long horse race that includes obstacles

superfluous: more than is necessary

ticker-tape parade: a celebratory parade in which tiny pieces of paper are showered on the honorees

tomboys: girls who have an interest in traditionally boy-centered activities

TO FIND OUT MORE

BOOKS

Gormley, Beatrice, and Meryl Henderson (illustrator). *Amelia Earhart: Young Aviator.* New York: Aladdin Paperbacks, 2000.

Howe, Jane Moore, and Cathy Morrison, (illustrator). *Amelia Earhart.* Carmel, Ind.: Patria Press, 2000.

Kerby, Mona. *Amelia Earhart: Courage in the Sky.* New York: Puffin, 1996.

Sloate, Susan. *Amelia Earhart: Challenging the Skies.* New York: Fawcett, 1995.

Szabo, Corinne, and Linda Finch. *Sky Pioneer: A Photobiography of Amelia Earhart.* Washington, D.C.: National Geographic Society, 1997.

Wood, Leigh Hope. *Amelia Earhart.* Broomall, Penn.: Chelsea House, 1996.

INTERNET SITES

Amelia Earhart: American Aviatrix
http://www.bena.com/lucidcafe/library/96jul/earhart.html
Information about Earhart and links to other figures in aviation.

Amelia Earhart Birthplace Museum
http://www.ameliaearhartmuseum.org/
Information about the museum as well as biographical details about Earhart.

Amelia Earhart Photos
http://www.atchison.org/Amelia/earhart grp1.html
Includes many interesting photographs of Amelia Earhart.

National Women's Hall of Fame: Amelia Earhart
http://www.greatwomen.org/erhrt.htm
A biography of Earhart plus information on many other famous women.

The Official Amelia Earhart Website
http://www.ameliaearhart.com/
Contains a biography and photo gallery of Earhart as well as a page of quotations and a timeline of her accomplishments.

Two Legends of Aviation
http://www.worldbook.com/fun/aviator/html/twolegend.html
To learn more about Amelia Earhart and Charles Lindbergh.

INDEX

About the Author

Lucia Raatma received her bachelor's degree in English literature from the University of South Carolina and her master's degree in cinema studies from New York University. She has written a wide range of books for young people. When she is not researching or writing, she enjoys going to movies, playing tennis, practicing yoga, and spending time with her husband, daughter, and golden retriever. She lives in New York.